Sales Enablement

The Framework for Sales and Marketing Collaboration

Jeff Nguyen

Copyright © 2022 by Jeff Nguyen

This document contains opinions and ideas of the authors. It is sold for the purpose of providing helpful and reliable information; the publisher, authors, and all other parties involved in the making of this document are not required to render any qualified services or advice.

The information provided herein is strictly for educational and entertainment purposes; any liability, in terms of inattention or otherwise, by any usage or abuse of any policies, processes, or directions contained within, is the solitary and utter responsibility of the reader.

The content and information contained in this book has been compiled from sources deemed reliable, and it is accurate to the best of the Author's knowledge, information and belief. However, the Author cannot guarantee its accuracy and validity and cannot be held liable for an-y errors and/or omissions. Further, changes are periodically made to this book as and when needed. Where appropriate and/or necessary, you must consult a professional (including but not limited to your doctor, attorney, financial advisor or such other professional advisor) before using any of the suggested remedies, techniques, or information in this book.

Under no circumstances will any legal responsibility or blame be held against the publisher, author, or any other parties involved in the making of this document for any reparation, damages, or monetary loss due to the information herein, either directly or indirectly. This disclaimer applies to any loss, damages or injury caused by the use and application, whether directly or indirectly, of any advice or information presented, whether for breach of contract, tort, negligence, personal injury, criminal intent, or under any other cause of action.

You agree to accept all risks of using the information presented inside this book.

Permission is not granted to reproduce, duplicate, or transmit any part of this document in electronic or printed format. Recording of this publication is also prohibited and storage of this document is not allowed without the written permission from the publisher.

All rights are reserved.

Contents

1. Introduction — 1
2. What is Sales Enablement? — 3
3. Ownership of Sales Enablement — 11
4. A Culture of Sales Enablement — 16
5. Preparing the Organization for Enablement — 24
6. Enablement, Onboarding, & Training — 41
7. Content Management — 51
8. Internal Communication — 63
9. Technology & Tools — 69
10. Conclusion — 79

Chapter One

Introduction

Sales enablement is a philosophy and practice of supporting sales teams with the tools, resources, and processes they need to be successful. It includes the building of a culture in which salespeople feel empowered to succeed. It also includes strategies for onboarding new hires and training them to be effective in their roles. The focus is on making sure that every individual in the company can identify what value they bring to the table--what role they play in helping salespeople be successful--so that each person can take ownership of his or her role.

The most important thing to remember about sales enablement is that it's not just about salespeople! It's about the customer experience, and everyone in the organization should be thinking about how they can help facilitate an ideal experience for customers.

A great way to think about sales enablement is as a set of infrastructure resources that are put into place to help the sales team reach their desired objectives.

At its core, this infrastructure includes things like content, training programs, and technology tools that allow salespeople to be better prepared for selling opportunities and make it easier for them to document the progress they've made in closing deals.

Sales enablement also includes the active involvement of leaders in other areas of the organization (like marketing or finance) who are responsible for driving certain aspects of the sales process through their own departments. These people often identify areas where they can improve on functionality or efficiency so that they can help salespeople do their jobs more effectively.

The goal of sales enablement is to ensure that the sales team is as effective as possible in their job. In order to do this, one must consider the needs of both the company and the sales team. There are many different aspects to sales enablement, including:

- Ownership of Sales Enablement

- Preparing the organization for enablement

- Enablement, Onboarding, & Training

- Content Management

- Internal Communication

- Technology & Automation

Throughout this book, we will examine each of the areas above as they relate to sales enablement.

Chapter Two

What is Sales Enablement?

What exactly is sales enablement?

Sales enablement is the practice of equipping sales teams with the tools they need to close more sales. In short, it's about helping salespeople sell better.

Though the term "sales enablement" has only been around for about a decade, the idea behind it has been around for much longer. In fact, sales have always been one of the most self-sufficient facets of any business. Salespeople are generally expected to learn their craft on the job or through some form of training, and they are usually left to rely on their own intuition when it comes to improving their skills.

But since 2013, when a Gartner report declared that sales enablement would be "the most important initiative to drive revenue growth," organizations have begun to realize that there's more than one way to reap bigger profits—and that sales people need help in order to capitalize on these other opportunities. Sales enablement is one way of providing this assistance: It places emphasis on revenue as the end result and puts processes in place that make it easier for salespeople to achieve that result.

Sales enablement provides these missing pieces through a variety of channels: from industry-specific research and data on target markets to eBooks geared toward helping salespeople improve in specific areas of their craft. Sales enablement can take many forms—from the written word (white papers, articles, eBooks) to video (webinars, podcasts) and even social media (blogs, Facebook posts).

Though many companies have their own ways of describing sales enablement, experts agree that the best way to explain it is as "software designed to improve sales staff interaction with customers by arming them with the knowledge and resources they need to satisfy customer needs." Sales enablement goes beyond training or consulting services; it's a complete system, from managing your leads to closing the deal. It's all about knowing your buyers' wants, needs and expectations and providing them with what they're looking for.

The Characteristics of Sales Enablement

The primary goal of sales enablement is easy to understand. It's all about equipping sales teams with the tools they need to succeed. It's a more nuanced conversation to talk about how to actually make this happen. A lot of focus often goes towards defining and building the right tools, but it can be equally if not more important to think about why you're building them in the first place. You want your sales team to be successful, but that can mean different things depending on who they are, what they're selling, and the context of your company's larger goals. Sales enablement is an opportunity to align sales goals with broader company objectives; it's a chance for you to help your sales team get closer to who you want them to be as a group and as individuals.

Second, the focus of sales enablement is on the customer, not the seller. Sales enablement is a process that empowers sellers with the tools they need to effectively communicate with their ideal customers, but it's important to remember that those ideal customers are at the heart of sales enablement. That means delivering these tools when and where the customers need them. You'll want to know when your buyers intend to use these assets. Remember: you're building solutions for your customers, not for your sales teams, so give them what they need (and don't forget about what they don't know they need).

When it comes to sales enablement, there are two distinct classes of content that are a regular part of the sales process: the stuff you'll hand over to your customer and the materials you use exclusively within your sales team. The former is usually in reference to data that's more specific to your product or service, things like case studies, videos, and detailed product sheets. The latter are more general resources that help your salespeople do their jobs better, such as guides, white papers, and checklists.

Enabling your sales team to succeed isn't just about their access to the right tools, it's also about ensuring they're familiar with them. A sales department should be continuously learning and developing, so that the people working in it are always equipped with the most up-to-date knowledge and skills. You need to create a culture of education and growth where everyone has access to new resources and is encouraged to seek out more. That way, you can make sure your people have all the information they need about your products and services, as well as any additional training or learning that will help them improve their results.

Fifth, to ensure that sales enablement helps its intended audience, you must ensure that the materials you provide to them are intuitive. Creating a user-friendly interface means making tools accessible and simple to use. The point here is to make sure there are repeated uses of these materials, as this can only happen if they are of high quality (refer back to the earlier point about understanding what buyers want) and easy to use.

Sixth, ensuring that sales training is not a one-and-done endeavor is crucial to ensuring your company's success. Sales enablement software that doesn't give you the ability to monitor how your sales team is using the material you provide will ensure that the time and effort you put into creating sales training materials is wasted. The ideal software can help you use data from your sales training efforts to improve future sales enablement initiatives, ensuring the most bang for your buck.

Seventh, the idea behind the implementation of sales enablement is that its features can be measured. Sales enablement metrics like average deal size, number of reps who hit quota, and length of sales cycle are all important to monitor. Not only are these three metrics important but they are also a good starting point for tracking other metrics. By knowing these three initial metrics you can determine which areas need improvement by comparing them against industry averages or competitors. Sales enablement is a process that has measurable results and helps to drive revenue growth goals both short and long term.

The Importance of Sales Enablement

Sales enablement is a highly effective way to improve the productivity of salespeople while also increasing revenue. The Aberdeen Group found that companies with company-wide adoption of best practices in sales achieved quota twice as often as their competitors. At the same time, 57% of sales representatives at companies with a sales enablement team met or exceeded their targets. All this points to the fact that an investment in sales enablement can have a huge impact on your business' bottom line.

The best programs engage employees and free up their time by having them develop content for themselves, and then share it internally. It's just one of the reasons that two-thirds of businesses who have a company-wide commitment to training are able to meet or exceed their revenue goals.

You should be thinking about sales enablement as an investment in your staff's future, and therefore, your organization's future. When you invest in sales enablement, you will see immediate benefits in your pipeline fill rates, conversion rates, and close ratios. You will see an increase in overall revenue and also a decrease in churn rate; all because you're empowering your team members to do what they do best: sell!

When you have a high-performing sales team, it's easy to think that the sales enablement program is unnecessary, as your salespeople are already doing great. However, as the number of people in your sales organization grows, you need to ensure that everyone has access to the same tools and education. A sales enablement program helps ensure that any new hire can hit the ground running in their ability to succeed in the job.

If you have a well-established sales department, it's easy for people to slip into complacency with their current methods of working. Sales enablement can help protect against this by making sure that everyone has access to the information and training they need to meet or exceed expectations.

Responsibilities of Sales Enablement

Sales enablement is a hot topic in the world of sales, and for good reason. It's an easy way to connect what the company does with what its salespeople are doing, and can be a great way to keep your team happy. Sales enablement gets you on common ground with your team, helping you to better lead them—but this is only possible if you take the time to get it right. There are so many things that go into making sure a sales enablement program is effective.

Carefully select your hires

To help make sure that your program is well-rounded and effective, always remember that talent and flexibility are often more important than experience when making hiring decisions. The most valuable workers are those who can adjust to new situations and take on new responsibilities accordingly. A new hire with a strong drive to learn can quickly catch up to and even surpass those with more experience within the first year on the job.

Establish Goals and Objectives

Every sales organization is unique, so there are very few universal truths about what the role of sales enablement should be in a given company. As a result, the best way to figure out what the sales enablement role is in your organization is to start by defining the goals and objectives you want it to achieve.

Experts recommends that you define the role as little as possible in terms of activities and as much as possible in terms of outcomes. If you outline a too rigid process to achieve results, you run the risk that:

1) people won't be able to use their initiative and creativity to find ways to make the process better, and

2) the process won't resonate with some people, leading to poor results.

As long as your team members have access to relevant data and resources, they'll know how they're doing along the way.

This isn't to say that you shouldn't give them some direction and advice—but ultimately let them figure out how to reach their destination on their own. You need to trust that they'll do something good with both your hard work and your advice. The right people will get it done without much guidance, but if they don't know where they're supposed to be going, they won't be able to get there.

Take Away Roadblocks

Sales enablement is the first line of defense in demonstrating that sales isn't an insurmountable black box. As the coach and trainer for your team, you're responsible for making sure they're equipped with all the resources they need to perform their jobs effectively, from product knowledge to effective sales skills.

However, your job as a sales manager doesn't end at providing them with this information. You must also ensure that your sales staff has access to it and can use it to their advantage when interacting with customers. When you create a stress-free setting for your sales team by establishing and promptly updating clear territories, compensation plans, holdout/transition rules, etc., you're taking away the roadblocks from their sightlines. With these distractions out of the way, they'll be better able to see what's in front of them: customers who are ready to buy.

At times, you may have to get involved and help them see what you're seeing—you have more experience managing teams than they do working directly with customers, so maybe you've noticed something they haven't yet picked up on—but ultimately, it's up to them how well they translate this information into positive results for the company.

Create The Right Culture

Sales enablement is the process of making sure that people inside a company have the tools and knowledge they need to sell. It's not just about training salespeople; it involves the entire company, from the boardroom to customer service, so that the sales tactics and messages are consistent across departments. Sales enablement encompasses different roles, but it's ultimately about motivating your staff to reach their full potential, so that every individual feels connected and inspired by his or her work.

The best sales enablement programs don't just respond to needs; they anticipate them. To do this, you'll want to start by determining what motivates your staff and its members to reach their full potential—not your potential. It's important to have a fair compensation plan, but it's also crucial to provide public recognition for excellent work. Numerous factors, including prosapects for professional growth, educational advancement, or the realization of personal goals, can influence an individual's level of motivation (or lack thereof).

And finally, it's paramount that you work for your team rather than thinking of them as "your employees." If you create the mentality that they're working for both of you rather than just themselves, then they will reciprocate by doing the same for everyone else on the team.

What Makes a Good Sales Enablement Plan?

Sales enablement is a big undertaking for any company, but particularly so for the ones that wish to outpace their competitors in the ever-changing landscape of business. Sales enablement calls for a blend of proven methods, both technological and human, that are so effective they can be used across multiple departments and on an ongoing basis.

It's not just one piece of equipment, piece of instruction, or procedure that makes sales enablement successful. This cocktail could consist of tools that help businesses implement processes and best practices, or it could be best practices that are delivered and then measured with the help of technology.

The success of sales enablement depends on this combination, which necessitates the participation of individuals from across the organization. The program must be supported by a solid infrastructure and the right tools, and it should be organized in a way that is easy to understand and follow.

Sales enablement requires the participation of multiple departments, including marketing, product management, legal and compliance, HR, and IT—for example, you need to have a system in place that allows your sales team to easily find information about new products and procedures as they become available. A highly-engaged sales team can increase revenue by as much as 500%, so it's worth taking the time to make sure your organization has a plan for ensuring sales enablement is always top-of-mind for everyone.

In order to create a successful strategy for sales enablement, you need to involve more than just your internal staff; you need a comprehensive strategy that incorporates all of these methods into a streamlined, repeatable process for your sales team. Stick with what works and don't get caught up in all the latest trends; focus on giving your team everything they need to succeed instead.

Chapter Three

Ownership of Sales Enablement

Many companies are beginning to rely on the use of software to enable sales reps' productivity, but so far there has not been a clear delineation of who owns sales enablement. Is it the part of sales operations? Or perhaps it's a function that is shared among the various departments involved in sales and marketing.

In most cases, it seems to be a loose collaboration between various stakeholders. But this approach introduces confusion over who is responsible for aligning the software platform with business objectives, and therefore which team needs to be involved in decisions about new features and releases. If sales leaders are not involved in these decisions, they may find themselves unable to adequately support their team members, or worse, become frustrated by the lack of functionality that impacts the success of their teams' performance.

To clarify ownership of sales enablement, a company must first define its goals and priorities for sales enablement software. The technology manager should then determine which department will serve as the single point of contact for all requests related to this area of software. This department will also handle any questions related to training and consulting services provided by the vendor as well as user adoption activities. It's also important to ensure that business goals drive new features and releases from both an IT standpoint as well as a sales enablement standpoint. This includes aligning on the different user personas and their specific needs, as well as determining how best to support them with your sales enablement software.

Sales Enablement and Sales Operations

Some companies choose to keep Sales Enablement and Sales Operations separate, but it makes the most sense to have them report to the same department.

The success of the sales team relies heavily on the efforts of both of these departments. Both departments share in the accountability for the sales team's success and are tasked with finding new ways to improve the sales force's productivity.

The information that sales receives as part of the sales enablement program is not fully useful until it is "operationalized" by sales operations.

Differences between sales operations and sales enablement

Sales operations and sales enablement are two terms that describe the same thing. Some companies have merged these departments into a single one, whereas others have kept them separate. But what's really important is the work that people in these departments do every day to help support your sales team. When you think about it, these roles are nothing more than an extension of your brand. They make sure that your company's reputation lives on even when you're not around to tell potential customers what a great product or service you have to offer. Sales enablement and sales operations people play a critical role in building internal relationships with the sales team, as well as working with outside partners like distributors and resellers who have a presence in the field.

Sales operations and sales enablement are both demanding roles that require a commitment to long-term goals, but they are not the same thing.

What are some of the main differences between sales operations and sales enablement? In my experience, one of the main distinctions is how far along in its maturity cycle your company is. If it's still fairly young or small, there may not be any formal separation between sales operations and sales enablement. In large organizations, though, where there might be multiple business units and many different products to sell across different market segments, it makes sense for each unit to be responsible for their own sales function—and thus their own dedicated sales operations and sales enablement teams.

Sales operations is the group within a company that is responsible for managing all aspects of sales, including day-to-day operations, quotas, bonuses, and compensation. Sales operations has the perspective of looking at the big picture to evaluate and manage processes that help increase profit over time. As a result of this long-term focus, sales operations often takes a more process-oriented approach to its work.

Sales enablement, on the other hand, focuses on providing information and resources to support salespeople in their day-to-day activities. It's focused on supporting people who are actively selling for an organization. Sales enablement's work is driven by an understanding of what makes each salesperson successful as an individual, which requires taking a long-term view of how each person learns and grows in their role.

Both groups have their own strengths and weaknesses; where they overlap is often where problems can arise. The conversation about whether one or both groups should be housed within a single department is ongoing. But we are seeing that companies with both functions report greater results than those who do not have them under one roof.

Sales Enablement and Marketing

Sales and marketing are, for the most part, completely separate entities. Salespeople are responsible for creating revenue by helping clients solve their problems and influence customers to purchase their products and services. Marketing professionals, on the other hand, are focused on increasing brand awareness, building customer demand, and establishing credibility through activities like paid advertising. With these differing goals in mind, it makes sense that they'd be separate departments with different responsibilities. The question is: should the sales and marketing departments work together?

In most cases, it seems to be a loose collaboration between various stakeholders. But this approach introduces confusion over who is responsible for aligning the software platform with business objectives, and therefore which team needs to be involved in decisions about new features and releases. If sales leaders are not involved in these decisions, they may find themselves unable to adequately support their team members, or worse, become frustrated by the lack of functionality that impacts the success of their teams' performance.

In more successful companies, the function of sales enablement is broken into two parts: sales operations and marketing enablement. Sales operations typically owns the development and publishing of content, while marketing enablement takes ownership of design, messaging, and curation. This can vary however based on company size and business model. There are times when marketing owns some or all content creation, or when sales operations owns design and messaging. It really depends on what's best for a particular organization.

At its core, sales enablement is about communication. It can include everything from creating a company-wide sales policy manual to developing a process for sharing sales reports to providing a collection of templates for common documents like meeting agendas and product brochures. It can also include things like training programs or webinars that teach new skills or make existing ones more effective.

When it comes to sales enablement and marketing, each department has something the other does not, and this is what makes them good partners. Marketing, for example, is concerned with the entire picture of an organization: who it is trying to reach, how it looks to those people and what kind of branding its message has. Sales is more concerned with specific details about a company's products or services: why consumers should buy from them and what benefits they receive from doing business with that company.

Marketing needs to be in charge when creating sales enablement materials because it understands the big picture. Sales needs to take charge when creating sales enablement materials because it understands the details. When marketing and sales work together, they can create a symbiotic relationship where each one benefits from the other's expertise.

Marketing can help sales with its messaging, while sales can help marketing with its expertise in the specifics of your company's offerings. When they work together, they create powerful tools that drive revenue.

Marketing and sales need each other to succeed.

Chapter Four

A Culture of Sales Enablement

Many companies, when faced with a drop in revenue, are quick to blame their sales teams. They figure, if no one's buying the product, then it's because the sales staff simply needs to be taught how to get the customers to buy. 95% of businesses spend money on sales training, but only 9% actually see a return on their investment.

In other words: most sales training doesn't work for most companies.

Sometimes this is true—if you have a bad product or an unenticing brand, then there may be nothing you can do to sell it. But more often than not, there are other factors at work in a declining revenue stream—the changing tastes of your customer base; increased competition from other businesses; or even the natural cycle of the economy—and it's important to unearth the real reasons for a drop in sales before you start pointing fingers at the people who deal with them every day: your sales team.

Salespeople are often considered the company's soul. They're the ones who face the market, the customers, and all of their feedback. They're the ones who hear about what could be done better—and who are expected to make it happen. And yet there's a big disconnect between sales and every other department at an organization. Sales teams often work from their own floor or building, in their own offices. It's a culture of isolationism that can easily lead to a "them vs. us" attitude, where sales think they have to be in charge of everything, when they should really only be accountable for one thing: revenue.

To combat this, sales should get involved with other departments, including customer success, account management, marketing, and others. Salespeople already spend a lot of time on trains or planes between appointments—why not use that time to build relationships with other people in the company? As anyone in business will tell you: communication is key. If salespeople are more involved with others around them, they'll better understand how they can improve their efforts and make suggestions that will benefit the company as a whole (and not just sales).

A culture of sales enablement is a self-sustaining environment in which sales teams can operate with the knowledge, resources, and support necessary to achieve their goals. It is characterized by a collaborative approach in which members of an organization continuously seek to improve their performance and develop each other through feedback, coaching, training programs, and mentoring relationships. The exchange of ideas is encouraged and rewarded. Salespeople are able to make decisions independently without fear of reprisal if they go against the status quo. There is no hesitation on management's part to empower employees with appropriate resources and information in order to make them successful.

A culture of sales enablement enables an organization to be successful. It fosters a sense of empowerment among its staff members that leads to greater productivity, employee retention, and overall job satisfaction. It also helps the organization maintain a competitive advantage by fostering an environment where innovation and creativity can thrive, rather than one that stifles employee engagement with top performers who may leave for greener pastures after having had enough of an impersonal working environment.

Sales enablement streamlines the dissemination of information, metrics, and data. It helps people get up-to-speed quickly so they can make informed decisions. It also helps them know when they need more information or resources to make those decisions. By having a culture where self-service is encouraged and supported by leaders, organizations can create a more empowered workforce that is better connected to the organization's goals. Sales enablement is not just about helping salespeople make more money; it is also about helping everyone in your organization work together more effectively.

Examine the Efficiency of Your Sales Team

Though most organizations have sales enablement teams that support their demand generation, the scope of these teams often stops at "sales enablement", i.e., providing salespeople with information and tools to be as successful as possible. What happens when you take a step back and look at your sales culture as a whole?

By taking a step back and examining the state of your sales culture as a whole, you're able to understand what's working and what isn't. This allows you to focus on the aspects of your sales environment that are missing, which you can then work on improving in much the same way that you would any other major initiative. The key here is to understand exactly what the desired outcome is so that you can tailor each of the changes you make accordingly.

The quality of your sales force is not only about the numbers, but about how well the members of that force are able to work together and coexist in the same ecosystem. It's about communication tactics, management styles, and internal dynamics. The good news is that there's still plenty of room for improvement, even if you're already doing well. The bad news is that it takes a lot more than just a process to improve these intangibles. Tackling this issue requires that you take a hard look at what's driving your sales team and how they interact with one another on both an individual and group level.

In order to create a culture where salespeople feel empowered to bring their A-game every single day, it's important to instill a sense of trust with them. You want them to know that they have the support and resources they need, not just from their manager but from the larger organization as well.

This can be a daunting task—but it can also be incredibly rewarding if you know where to start.

Decide How to Evaluate Sales Enablement Success

One of the most important aspects of effective sales enablement is making sure that the way you measure success is aligned with the culture of your company and the day-to-day activities of your salespeople. It's possible to get a good sense of how well sales enablement is doing its job simply by identifying what the goals are at each stage of the sales process, then measuring how often each goal occurs.

Companies often have inefficiencies in their sales processes that can be costly if dealt with too late. Sales enablement makes up for these inefficiencies by providing tools and resources to support the sales team, saving them time and money. Salespeople who are properly enabled are more efficient at closing deals, which means more revenue for the company overall.

One of the most important things a business can do is to make an explicit decision about whether success metrics for sales enablement will be based on salespeople's use of content or based on the results they see from sales enablement programs (such as closed deals or increased sales efficiency). It's also crucial to determine what types of systems will provide the data necessary for measurement, so progress can be tracked, analyzed, and improved upon over time.

It's important to use data to make sure your sales enablement efforts are working, but it's also important to have a plan in place for what you'll do once you've decided that sales enablement isn't doing what it's supposed to. It's possible that your sales enablement strategy is working well, but the people responsible for implementing it aren't doing so effectively. It's also possible that your sales enablement strategy isn't working well, and the problem lies in how it was designed rather than who is executing it. If you don't have a concrete way of measuring success and you're relying on intuition or guesses about the efficacy of your efforts, you may be able to identify problems before they get out of hand—or even before they happen at all.

Encourage Marketing to Communicate with Sellers

The best sales teams consistently report strong or outstanding collaboration with their marketing counterparts. According to a research study by Aberdeen Group, the top performers are more likely to have a culture of sales enablement than their weaker counterparts. This means that they encourage marketing to communicate with sellers on a regular basis, and establish policies that make it easier for salespeople to get in touch with those who can help them find opportunities.

The data is clear: creating a culture of sales enablement can help companies build stronger relationships between sales and marketing, and ultimately boost revenue. But how do you go about fostering such a relationship?

The most obvious way to do this is to make sure your sales and marketing teams are talking to each other. In fact, according to a recent survey, 75% of respondents said they believe they could increase their revenues if they simply did more cross-departmental communications.

You can make this easier by having a central place where both teams can go to access relevant information. In addition, you should also ensure that there is a balance in how much information marketing gives sales versus how much sales gives to marketing. Having a one-sided conversation will only hinder collaboration between your departments.

This doesn't mean you need to treat your marketing team like an arm of the sales department (or vice versa); instead, it means making sure that your team understands how their work impacts their colleagues' ability to sell successfully.

Improve Understanding of Customers Between Sales and Marketing

When we talk about sales enablement, we're talking about facilitating the process of selling rather than just helping sales people succeed in the act of selling. We want to ensure the success of the sale by removing obstacles from the process, and that means defining a culture that sets up a foundation for success through creating a shared understanding of customers. This can be done by developing a deeper understanding of customer context through shared experiences.

The division of labor is reflected in the division of labor that results from having separate dashboards. Marketing has its own tools and reports; Sales has its own tools and reports; and they never really talk to one another except when there's an issue with lead management or it's time to go over quarterly goals. These interactions are usually centered around numbers—how many leads did you get this month? How much did you spend on your campaign? What was your close rate?

By the time a lead has been nurtured through our nurturing program, all the relevant information that marketing and sales need to do their jobs well—including the contact's interests, social graphs, and even how they've interacted with our content—should be available in a single place. But our teams have often failed to work together to bring these insights into one place.

As a result, each team sees only part of the picture. By focusing solely on their individual tools for tracking leads, each department ends up missing out on critical information about the lead's context from the other perspective. Sales can't see what marketing has been doing to nurture a lead, and marketing can't see how sales is handling a given lead or what objections the sales team is encountering.

This splintering of knowledge is reflected in a common scenario we see in which marketing engages with a lead, does some nurturing via email or content, and at some point stops being able to make contact with them because they've moved into sales' territory.

Marketers are responsible for anticipating buyer needs and preferences, and then creating content that speaks to both. When we're able to provide Sales with a complete picture of each prospect's interests, problem statements and buying contexts, there's less back-and-forth between departments.

We accomplish this by keeping our Sales team's dashboards up-to-date with information about leads. For example, lead activity tracking through tools offers marketers insight into which content a lead has consumed, how they absorb it and what they do with it afterward. This can be used to create a CRM profile that gives Sales a unified view of each lead's developing interests and context for both departments.

By giving everyone in both departments access to all of the data from both perspectives, we're able to facilitate a deeper understanding of our customers' needs—and understand how we can meet them more effectively.

Celebrate Wins Together

If you have a sales and marketing team, their efforts should be celebrated together. Sales teams are measured by their performance on revenue targets, so they're most interested in how to grow those numbers. Marketing teams are measured by their ability to improve sales, so they're more interested in how to retain customers and convert new ones.

In order for success to be sustainable, teams need to be able to see the big picture at all times. Sales enablement is about improving the efficiency of salespeople, but it's also about raising their awareness of the work that marketing is doing on their behalf. The way I see it, everyone is working toward the same goal—making more money and spending less of it—and the best way to do that is by keeping your customers happy.

To encourage this type of relationship, marketing and sales should compile a report summarizing their accomplishments at the end of each month or quarter. When you document your team's progress, make sure you highlight any obstacles you faced and how you overcame them. If a campaign didn't perform as well as expected, find out what could have been done differently. If a vendor was late with your order or if the promotion wasn't as effective as it could have been, take note of what went wrong so you can learn from it for the next time around.

This is an opportunity for both teams to celebrate their wins together rather than keeping them separate. The key to making this meeting successful is to make sure it's not formal or "boring," as some review meetings can become. The purpose of this gathering is to get people from different divisions thinking together so that everyone leaves with a clearer picture of where they fit in and how they can make a difference.

Discussing these issues with your employees will reveal whether there are any holes in your marketing strategy or problems with your vendors that need to be addressed before they become bigger issues. The key thing is that everyone needs to be able to put their heads together when something goes wrong to figure out how to fix it. This is a very effective way to build teamwork and communication among your employees.

Making this meeting interesting and enjoyable will increase attendance, which in turn will improve retention of information and morale. After the meeting is over, everyone should mingle and toast the month's successes, with sales praising marketing for new content releases and marketing applauding sales for new SQLs or leads.

Chapter Five

Preparing the Organization for Enablement

Sales enablement is a critical component of an effective sales team, but there's no one-size-fits-all approach to getting it right. The way sales enablement is implemented varies by industry and company type, with some companies using more than one model to reach their goals.

Optimized sales enablement can reduce training costs, help your sales team close more deals, and increase the likelihood of new hires sticking around. A robust sales enablement program works best when it's tailored to the needs of your employees, industry, and company type.

There are many different models for how sales enablement is implemented in different organizations. Some companies use one model to support their entire sales force, while others use multiple models based on the needs of different territories or departments within their organization.

Best Practices for your Sales Enablement Program

To make sure you're getting the most out of your sales enablement, here are five key best practices to keep in mind.

1. Clearly articulate your program's intended outcomes.

2. Build sales enablement around the buyer's journey.

3. High-quality content should be produced and used extensively.

4. Never stop working on your sales training.

5. Ensure your sales staff is taking advantage of the resources you provide.

Clearly articulate your program's intended outcomes.

The first step in preparing for your sales enablement program is to clearly articulate its intended outcomes. Everyone involved should know where the program's going and what skills it will equip them with—and "improving sales performance" is too vague to be a useful answer.

By highlighting the most important skills for your sales team and then aligning your programs accordingly, you're setting everyone up for success. You want all of your salespeople to walk away from training with clear ideas of what they should be doing differently in order to boost their performance.

When deciding which skills to focus on, start by listing the skills that your salespeople need to be successful. Once you've identified the most important ones, think about how those skills can be developed, and consider the tools and resources that will help them learn. It's really important to understand what your sales reps need to do their jobs better, so try to get a sense of where they're coming from before making any assumptions. A good way to do this is by surveying your sales force and asking them what they'd like you to teach them. The best part about doing this is that you will also find out what your sales reps already know, so you'll have a better idea of how much time to spend on each skill.

The top salespeople in your company have some great ideas; why not hear them out? How about honing skills like public speaking to increase sales? There's no reason to settle on just one of these viable alternatives. And if you're concerned about budget, there are plenty of ways to implement a successful program without breaking the bank.

Build sales enablement around the buyer's journey.

Since sales enablement is all about helping sellers connect with customers, it makes sense to focus on improving the buying process. If you can improve the buying process and close deals more often, everybody wins.

This process starts with having a firm grasp on your buyer persona. This is an opportunity to get inside the heads of your customers and determine what they need to reach their goals.

An effective buyer persona will do more than just inform your message; it will also help you map out the buyer's journey and give you information on how to tailor your sales training and plays to each stage of the customer's path to purchase.

Buyer personas help organizations define their ideal demographic. They include a wealth of information about a company's potential clients, including information about their values, needs and concerns. With this knowledge in hand, businesses can create effective sales training and sales plays that will resonate with their customers; they also avoid wasting time and money on materials that don't appeal to the intended audience.

Once you have a solid understanding of who you're trying to sell to, it's time to take some steps toward improving their experience. This is where sales enablement comes into play. Not only does it continue to help you refine your message, but it also helps you develop successful sales plays that can be used in concert with new knowledge of the buying process to boost conversion rates for each step of the buyer's journey.

High-quality content should be produced and used extensively.

Content plays a vital role in sales enablement, but it often doesn't get the attention it deserves. Today's successful salespeople don't just rely on their own product knowledge and expertise of the industry. Sales departments that want to grow need to have a wide variety of high-quality content on hand that can be referred to by salespeople as they work with buyers.

Sales teams typically have different needs at every stage of the buying cycle: for instance, at the beginning stages of a sale, a buyer will likely have questions about whether a product or service will meet their needs, so educational content on those topics is necessary.

Later in the process, however, the buyer will likely be ready for more strategic insights into how your product or service can help them solve their problems—at that point in the process, you'll want to make sure your salespeople are providing valuable advice based on experience.

Sales Enablement should put time, effort, and money into building a fantastic library of relevant content. This will not only increase the value of your salespeople, but also decrease the amount of time and energy they have to spend on creating content.

Never stop working on your sales training.

Sales enablement training is about making sure every sales professional has the information and tools to be as successful as possible. It's also about knowing your audience and providing them with the right resources.

In today's world, business is conducted online and offline. Salespeople need to be prepared to deliver pitches and close deals wherever customers may be found. Sales enablement should prepare salespeople for this type of environment. Employers must cover all bases when it comes to providing quality sales training materials that can be accessed at any time by on-the-go professionals.

If a company doesn't make an effort to provide adequate sales training resources, its employees will not have access to critical information they need to succeed in their job. A lack of sales training can become a liability for a business if employees don't have up-to-date knowledge about products, pricing models, payment processing platforms, and customer service procedures.

A well-designed training program can also help land new recruits because prospective employees will see it as an indication that the company values its employees' learning experiences and growth opportunities.

This type of program should not only be ongoing but also interactive. Technology can help facilitate this process so that trainees feel more engaged. This will keep everyone up-to-date on sales enablement efforts throughout the year. Another option is to provide links to YouTube videos or short podcasts from professionals who are sharing their expertise on certain topics related to your sales training program, such as how to handle objections effectively during a presentation. These short video clips will help keep the trainees engaged and interested in learning more about sales and the industry itself.

Ensure your sales staff are using the resources you provide.

Ensuring that the sales team is taking advantage of the resources you provide is no small task. With such a wide variety of resources available, starting up any new sales enablement program can be a challenge. Even once it's off the ground, keep in mind that salespeople each have their own preferences, and they may resist what you think is the most effective method of communicating information.

If you've gone to the trouble of creating an organized sales enablement program, you don't want it to go to waste. Your salespeople need to understand and embrace the program as a whole, and use every tool at their disposal to maximize their results.

To that end, management needs to be sure that all aspects of sales enablement are being taken advantage of. Sales representatives must be familiar with your sales training materials, and they need to be taking full advantage of your sales support staff—by following up within the time allotted for them to do so after a meeting, for example. They should also be making effective use of any data or analytics resources you provide, whether that means using a CRM system effectively or making good use of your sales data visualizations.

In general, management needs to stay on top of what's going on in order to make sure that the tools provided are relevant and everyone is using it. Without someone keeping an eye on how sales makes use of what's provided to them, even the best sales enablement programs can fail. Sales management must insist that all members of the sales team use only the most effective methods, materials, and information.

Sales Tools and Software for Enablement

Sales enablement is more than just investing in technology and learning tools. In fact, most sales enablement programs fail because they don't incorporate technology, or do so without a cohesive strategy in place. By focusing on analytics and the organization's overarching goals, organizations can build a sales enablement culture that supports improved business results.

The ability to measure the effectiveness of your sales enablement program is critical for tying the program to business objectives. The first step is to define success measures tied directly to the organization's strategic objectives and business challenges. This process should be led by senior leadership and involve key stakeholders from across the organization working together to identify the most important goals for a given year. After these goals are identified, sales enablement must focus on tracking and continuously iterating on these metrics throughout the year.

With this information in hand, sales enablement organizations can determine what types of data they need to collect to drive that improvement. They can then use that data as part of identifying opportunities for improvement within their existing sales enablement resources and processes.

Obtain backing from upper management

It's very important to secure the backing of upper management and sales leadership before you begin taking steps to establish your new division. The success of your organizational efforts will be highly dependent on the credibility and visibility of your new group, and that in turn depends on how well you manage stakeholders' expectations. You should be aware of how you will contribute to their goals, how you will make their jobs easier, how you will support sales, and where they can help in return. Before spending any money or hiring anyone, you should get buy-in from the key people who have a lot of influence on your group's success.

Getting everyone on board from the start is especially critical if you're creating a standalone sales enablement department. In this case, you'll need every person in a position of power to help create an environment that welcomes this new initiative. This might include upper management, sales managers, sales teams, marketers, product managers, and more. Just as it's important to know what kind of relationships you want to form with these groups when trying to generate support for creating your own department—the relationship between departments must not only be collaborative but also transparent.

Ways to get the ball rolling include:

1.Make sure you've received permission to establish a sales enablement team. This step is key, as without it, you won't be able to move forward.

2.Reach out to executives and everyone else involved in the sales process—the more people know about your goals and how you plan to achieve them, the more likely they are to become advocates of your program.

3.Be sure there's communication between stakeholders in different departments and areas of the organization. Sales enablement isn't just about sales managers; it involves all of those who can help facilitate effective cross-department communication.

4.Don't wait until the last minute! You'll need time and flexibility to work with stakeholders to ensure that everyone's on board and playing their part, so don't put off reaching out until everything is ready to go.

Make Content Work for You

When sales representatives need to interact with target account contacts, they should be prepared to provide the buyers with something of value during the interaction. Value is typically provided through the use of content—whether it's content that marketing creates or content that sales reps are given as part of sales enablement training, it can be shared within your buyer's internal organization to help build a business case and demonstrate value.

When done well, content sharing during an interaction will not only build trust between your company and your buyer, but it will also help you boost your relationship with the buyer and increase the likelihood of getting a deal that closes. It's important to note that this requires a high level of business acumen on behalf of all involved parties across your company—but if everyone is able to work together to achieve this, sales enablement will be incredibly valuable for everyone involved.

Closing the deal isn't the end-all, be-all of your interactions with your buyer. Interactions should also serve as opportunities for you to influence future decisions and cultivate a long-term relationship with your prospect. When you're able to help them win internal battles, you'll come out ahead in the long run. Helping them create an internal business case for their initiative demonstrates value and sets up your sales organization for continued success in the future.

This type of content can take many forms: datasheets, videos, white papers, blog posts, dynamic landing pages, or even phone calls or emails. But when it comes down to it, each one is still a form of content. And while these tools are often created by marketing teams and shared by sales reps with prospects as a way to highlight specific products or services on behalf of the brand, they're not the only ways you can use content as a tool.

Improve Follow Up Cadence with Clients

All of a B2B sales team's efforts are directed toward engaging in dialogue with influential decision-makers—they're constantly researching their company, tracking the key executives' whereabouts or business trends and networking at industry events in order to connect on a personal level. Research conducted by The Bridge Group found that phone-centric sales teams have 26% more quality conversations per day than email-centric sales teams. A salesperson's ability to have productive phone conversations with key decision makers is directly correlated to the effectiveness of the tools they use.

Sales teams that operate more efficiently and engage in more quality conversations per day can have a significant competitive advantage. One way to achieve higher efficiency and more productive dialogues is through sales enablement tools.

Because even the most diligent salespeople aren't tracking their own sales statistics, many companies are not able to reach their full potential. This is because salespeople are often flying blind when it comes to improving their cold calling and lead generation techniques. Because of this gap in data collection, these companies lose out on valuable analytics that could help them make better decisions about how to grow sales in the future.

Salespeople can increase the quantity of phone calls they have with key clients by increasing their follow-up cadence. Using call analytics software makes it easy for sales representatives to see which hours of the day are most popular for making calls - this information can help reps plan their days around these peak call times. Call analytics software can also be used to automate the research process and optimize workflow, making it 4 times more likely for salespeople to follow up with leads.

Transparency in Sales Enablement

Sales enablement is one of the most powerful ways to ensure that everyone in the company is aware of how sales is doing and how potential clients and customers are behaving. It's important to work towards this company-wide effect on revenue. More suggestions, reactions, and alterations will be coming your way. It's everyone's job to make sales. Non-sales personnel, such as marketing, customer success, support teams, account management, and others, interact with potential customers at various points in the buying process. The importance of sales enablement being ingrained in the company's ethos should be made clear to everyone there.

In order to make sales enablement an effective effort throughout the organization, it needs to be well-communicated from top to bottom. Communication must be direct and frequent—this isn't just another initiative or project that can be put aside for a rainy day or for "later", after you've finished your other goals. Sales enablement needs to be a constant presence throughout every department and team, like air conditioning during the summertime. There needs to be a sense of urgency about sharing information among colleagues.

In a study done by SiriusDecisions and CEB, it was found that a lack of communication between sales and marketing is one of the most common problems businesses encounter when trying to improve lead quality. The study found that 54% of companies reported that there wasn't enough communication between the two departments about the status of leads, while 52% reported a lack of communication around lead definitions.

Sales Enablement can help here by making sure sales leadership and other departments are aware of the value marketing adds to the sales process and that they understand how their decisions affect sales effectiveness. Sales enablement can also be used to help explain why marketing makes certain requests or asks for certain resources, which would make everyone's jobs easier.

Measuring Performance in Sales Enablement

Sales enablement companies rely on a variety of metrics to assess sales rep performance and the health of their business. At the most basic level, they all want to know whether the reps are actually doing their job and what's holding them back. But as sales enablement efforts mature and more sophisticated sales processes are put in place, managers look for more specific information—they want to know whose accounts are being developed and which reps are closing more deals than they did last quarter, while still maintaining a high degree of customer service. It's these metrics that make sales enablement a more agile entity compared to traditional sales management.

When measuring performance, you will still want to report sales results in aggregate (after all, quotas are often set company-wide) but you should also break out those results by each individual salesperson. This will give you the ability to see which members of your team are truly effective and hold the others accountable for their performance.

Each member of a sales team can have access to their own personalized dashboard of metrics, complete with peer comparisons. This way, each rep can see how they're performing against their goals for the month and where exactly they are losing time in their days. For instance, your sales team might have a goal of "closing 3 deals," but if you don't consider that reaching this goal requires 7 hours of prospecting and 6 hours of consultative selling, your entire sales staff will be off target.

When you choose the wrong metrics, you won't be measuring what actually matters; your sales team's performance will not accurately reflect its true strengths and weaknesses. "Overall win rate" is a good example of a flawed metric: while it focuses attention on the most important aspect of winning deals (closing), it's not the only thing that matters. What if one salesperson closed more big deals than their peers but wasted a lot of time chasing leads that didn't pan out? It'd be better to focus on closed revenue instead: it tells you how much money you've brought in from new business rather than how many deals you've closed.

Key Metrics for Sales Enablement

It is absolutely crucial that the sales enablement strategies your company employs are effective and appropriate for the goals you have set. The only way to determine this is to evaluate the correct metrics.

Sales Cycle Length

Knowing how long your sales cycle is gives you insight into how effective (or ineffective) your sales process is as a whole. Sales reps can use this metric as a benchmark to assess their own performance, and managers can use it to help them figure out where problems are in the process.

An abnormally long sales cycle for a given product might indicate that some of your customers don't understand how to use it, or what benefits they'll get from using it. This is especially true if you're selling high-tech products.

A really short sales cycle has two possible interpretations: either the product is extremely easy to sell, which means that it might not be as complex as you think, or your sales team may only succeed with a few customers who are most likely to buy.

This information also helps you look forward: if your sales cycle length is growing, you're gaining more customers or acquiring them faster, but if it's shrinking, you might need to reevaluate the effectiveness of existing methods.

Target Attainment

Quota attainment is a measure of success for any sales team. For sales enablement to be successful, it must complement other tactics that help salespeople achieve their goals. A dashboard is a useful tool for monitoring the performance of your sales team and identifying knowledge gaps that may be preventing them from reaching their quotas. When your company is increasing its quota attainment, rather than just a few exceptional sales reps whose win rate has recently gone through the roof, the company is actually succeeding.

What's important about this metric is that it can determine whether or not your company will reach its quota, which could very well affect its revenue and overall success. If you see that your team members aren't attaining their goals—or even if they are, but they're just not performing well in comparison to other members of the organization—you may need to take steps to help them improve or encourage them to look for other jobs if they aren't happy with where they are.

Call to Actions

Despite the fact that not all call-to-actions (CTAs) will yield the same results, tracking them all is crucial.

The effectiveness of CTAs in your company's sales enablement strategies is revealed by a sales analysis. There are several ways to measure the effectiveness of your sales enablement content. You can track CTAs, conversion rates, time on page and bounce rate, but don't neglect tracking actual sales by using a CRM. You should also keep an eye on the quality of leads coming in through your content; if they're not qualified enough to move forward with sales, then it's not worth continuing with them.

The final stage of the sales funnel is crucial, so it's important to test different calls to action to determine which ones are most effective and then use those.

Contribution of Marketing

This metric is crucial because it reveals whether or not your marketing materials are helping you train your staff and provide excellent customer service.

As a sales enablement and training strategy, providing your sales team with marketing materials helps unify the team's efforts. However, this strategy will only work if you provide materials at every step of the buyer's journey, so that they have something to present to their customers at every decision point.

Marketing materials enable sales and support staff to educate customers and prospects about what your products can do for them, but without feedback from the sales team, it's impossible to know if the materials are effective in doing this.

Sales and support teams are the only ones who can tell you if the materials help close deals, and that makes their opinions invaluable.

Sales Process Compliance

Your company's success depends on your sales team following the established sales procedures rather than taking a shot in the dark or adopting their own processes.

To help close more deals and ensure your sales team is on the right track, consider including dependable sales processes in your sales enablement strategies that your sales teams can use on a daily basis to help close more deals. Your sales team will have everything they need to close deals thanks to a well-thought-out sales process.

If you don't track how well your salespeople are following processes, you run the risk of them shortchanging customers in their interactions. If a customer needs something specific to move forward with a deal and your sales rep doesn't provide it—because they didn't know to ask, or because they forgot—you could lose that potential sale. It's important to keep tabs on whether your team is providing customers with everything they need to make sound decisions (I'm sure you've all been in meetings where someone asks a question that seems obvious after the fact).

Whether done automatically by software or manually by sales reps, this measurement keeps everyone on the same page.

Sales Conversion Rate

Sales conversion rate is the most important metric to track in a sales enablement strategy. This metric is the ratio of customers who accepted proposals to the total number of proposals made. The lower this ratio is, the more likely it is that you need to adjust your sales enablement strategies.

If you're tracking other metrics, like lead generation or proposal responses, you can also see how close each lead gets to becoming a customer by comparing it with your conversion rates. A low conversion rate could indicate that all leads aren't being turned into proposals in a timely manner and that some are falling through the cracks entirely. So if you notice that your sales closing ratio is higher than your conversion rate, you know that something must be going wrong in the proposal-response process. This can allow you to easily identify where things are slowing down so you can make adjustments before more customers slip away.

Win Percentage

A win/loss ratio can be calculated by dividing the number of wins by the total of all losses, with either a percentage or fractional value. According to Investopedia, this ratio is useful in comparing your sales team's performance against your competitors' and in assessing the effectiveness of various sales enablement strategies.

A rising win rate indicates that your sales team is getting better at closing deals, but a declining win rate may indicate that something needs to change in order for your company to stay competitive. Sales enablement tools like relevant content can help by spreading awareness about new products, services, and features. This will give prospects the necessary background on which to base their buying decisions, which will in turn increase the likelihood of a sale.

Using this strategy effectively: As with many other sales enablement strategies, this approach works best when it's paired with an effective software solution.

Onboarding Time

Onboarding time is a great place to start understanding how quickly your sales enablement is working. Onboarding time is the time it takes for your new hires to get accustomed to the job and begin producing for you. Rapid onboarding is evidence that your sales enablement strategies are working. It's easier to bring on board new customers when they have access to all the information they need at the right time.

A high score on this metric indicates that your marketing materials are providing your customers with all the information they need to make informed buying decisions. This metric cannot be ignored because it will help you save time in the long run by preventing your sales team from having to ask basic questions during their onboarding process. Tracking employee adoption rates will help you fine-tune sales enablement and quicken the transition if necessary. When managers only need to check in with new hires occasionally, they save both time and money.

Deal Size

A crucial element of sales enablement is determining the value of deals that your company has closed. It's important to have a way to keep track of this information because it allows you to easily spot trends and measure the success of your marketing programs.

When you experience success, take the time to analyze it so that you can learn from and apply those lessons in future opportunities. Aligning your marketing and sales departments to develop upsell and cross-sell strategies can help you close deals with a higher total value.

The value of your deals reflects how well your sales team communicates with customers and conveys your brand's message and value. Analyze the average size of each deal so that you can target larger clients.

Chapter Six

Enablement, Onboarding, & Training

Onboarding is the process of orienting new hires to a company and its culture. This means introducing them to all aspects of your organization—the products, the sales strategy, and the general approach.

Onboarding is most crucial in the first three months on the job, when new hires must be immersed in their team's culture and mission. But onboarding doesn't end there: it must continue for the first ninety days, when your employers need to be educated on your products, sales strategy, and general approach. The value of a good onboarding process is obvious—it was estimated that 50% of all senior hires do not stay in their position longer than 18 months and 50% of all hourly workers do not stay longer than 3 months, with 25% of the workforce experiencing a career transition annually.

Moreover, if a new hire has a positive onboarding experience, they are nearly 60% more likely to remain with your company for at least three years.

The Scope of Onboarding

When you're considering onboarding, it's important to remember that "onboarding" encompasses much more than a simple orientation for new employees to your company (although orientation is often an important aspect of onboarding). As the American Society for Training and Development defined it in 2013, "Onboarding is the process of helping new hires adjust to the social and performance aspects of their job quickly and smoothly." This definition includes not just social and cultural integration, but also learning the necessary knowledge and skills for success at work.

A company's onboarding process is designed to acclimate new hires to their new environment, but the scope of this process should vary depending on the needs of each business. With the ultimate aim of bridging the gap between company-wide goals and day-to-day tasks, an onboarding plan should zero in on what matters most to each department. For example, a new sales representative may be trained in his or her primary duties, but also should be made aware of how their success feeds into the larger goals of the organization.

Sales enablement training must go beyond a review of sales processes and procedures; it is essential that employees understand how they fit into the overall company structure. This is why a comprehensive onboarding plan should include both soft skills and hard skills training. While the former may seem less important than the latter, it is often the case that employees who fail to grasp basic business concepts will have difficulty making an impact on their teams.

In fact, many experts define onboarding as being split into three separate components: social integration, knowledge transfer, and performance support.

Social integration might include helping new hires know how to act in different situations (e.g., sitting in on a meeting before you're allowed to speak), understanding the norms of your workplace culture (e.g., what's appropriate attire for the office), or getting to know coworkers and making friends with them.

Knowledge transfer involves teaching your new hire how to do their job responsibilities—this could be specific tasks, or it could involve sharing key knowledge about your company's history, mission statement, or culture.

Performance support includes helping new hires understand what they need to do to succeed at their job. This could mean setting up new employees with a mentor or providing them with training on how to use certain software programs.

Support during transition includes helping new hires adjust to their new role, whether it's through mentorship or simply by making sure they have everything they need (e.g., equipment or supplies).

Onboarding vs. Orientation

Orientation is a one-time occasion where new employees are formally welcomed to the company. They'll learn about the company's history, its policies, and their new colleagues. Most importantly, they'll receive a list of tasks that need to be completed in order to ensure a smooth transition into their role. Orientation is the period of time when new employees are getting familiar with the expectations and standards of their organization—having everything from how to file paperwork to what kind of technology they'll be using at their fingertips can go a long way toward helping them feel prepared for their new position.

Onboarding, on the other hand, is a continuous process. It's intended to help employees keep up with their learning after they've already been hired, and it includes processes like training, mentoring, and ongoing feedback on performance.

A formal orientation program gives new employees the tools they need to be successful as quickly as possible. This is especially relevant in job areas that require a large amount of training—engineering, for example—or in companies with strict hiring standards. New employees need to learn everything from the company's mission and structure to their daily tasks and the names of everyone they'll be working with. While some aspects of this can be passed on informally by team members and managers, a structured orientation program ensures that all important information is communicated clearly and completely.

Training vs. Onboarding

Although training is a vital part of the onboarding process, the first 90 days are where the real work gets done. There is no doubt that onboarding and training go hand in hand, but you should know that training is distinct from onboarding due to the focus on learning the specifics of one's job duties.

The scope of onboarding should be carefully considered as it goes far beyond learning how to use an e-mail client or how to conduct oneself in formal settings. Onboarding should include an introduction to company culture, ethics, and history as well as an overview of all programs including compensation, benefits, insurance, and time off, among others. While these factors are all essential parts of any employee's life in your organization, they require dedicated attention throughout the onboarding process in order to avoid confusion and prevent misunderstandings. Your onboarding program should include a review of employee handbooks and policies as well.

The onboarding phase of a new employee's career is a crucial time to begin establishing rapport with the worker. The work ethic of the quality candidates you've identified will be cemented and a positive work environment will be established if this system of support is put in place early on. It will be much more challenging for your new hires to connect with the organization on a fundamental level if there is no pillar of company ethics supporting the training.

Training focuses on improving the skill and knowledge of your employees. Corporate training, such as regular sessions on team processes or presentations from the executive team, are a part of this. But so are employee-led sessions on specific features or aspects of individual products that may have changed recently. In sales enablement, these types of sessions are often called "sales focused," because they're geared toward providing sales teams with the insight they need to be successful in their day-to-day efforts.

Training sometimes focuses on other areas as well, such as compliance requirements or internal policies that might not seem directly related to sales. This type of training is still beneficial for your employees, but it should be scheduled in a separate location or time from "sales focused" activities in order to avoid confusion.

Training vs. Enablement

Sales training and sales enablement are two categories used to describe different methods companies use to help sales teams be as productive as possible. However, these two approaches are often confused with one another. Sales enablement is a group of resources that helps salespeople do their job, such as sales tools, sales training, and quota management. Sales training is a set of strategies that helps salespeople close deals, such as onboarding and quotas. In short, sales enablement provides the tools and the means by which to use them effectively; sales training provides the strategies that help your people close those deals.

Sales Enablement is the process of ensuring that sales representatives and managers are equipped with the resources to do their jobs effectively. It is an umbrella term for all of the resources, content, and tools that a company makes available to its sales team. Sales training is more focused on providing instruction to reps and managers through classroom or virtual training sessions. Both are crucial parts of a company's strategic sales plan—together they ensure that sales representatives have everything they need to succeed.

Sales training can take many forms, including one-on-one coaching, group sessions with peers, and credentialing initiatives. Providing ongoing training for your sales team is just as important as the initial training provided to new hires.

One-on-one coaching is an excellent way to help sales reps develop their skills from a new perspective and can be a great way to fill any knowledge gaps that may have been overlooked during the initial training process.

Group sessions with peers are also a great way for sales reps to learn from other members of the sales team who may have some specific strengths in areas like soft skills or closing techniques.

Certification programs are often overlooked as part of sales training, but they're an excellent way to reinforce the skills learned during initial training and throughout ongoing coaching.

Sales readiness is a term used to describe a sales team's ability to effectively communicate with customers, understand their needs and help them reach the decision to buy. In order to be ready for the sales process, a sales team must have the proper training and tools and resources (enablement) that are available for any given situation in the field.

Training for Improved Sales Enablement

Training your organization is all about improving sales effectiveness. At the core of that is effective sales enablement.

The importance of creating buyer personas

To succeed, salespeople need to understand the motivations and interests of their prospects. To do this, they must be able to imagine themselves as the buyer, and that requires a good grasp of what motivates buyers to make decisions.

Which is why it's so crucial for salespeople to learn about buyer personas. Buyer personas are fictional representations of your ideal customers: By understanding who these buyers are and what makes them tick, not only do you know more about their needs, but you also have a better understanding of how to appeal to them.

Salespeople can gain a deeper insight into their target market by using buyer personas. But this type of training isn't just for the sales team—it's also important for those who work in marketing or product development because it helps them understand what needs to be included in the product or service they're selling, and how best to communicate that information.

It's also possible that buyers come from a wide variety of industries. For example, you might have one persona who represents your company's CEO and another who represents the owner of an e-commerce shop—both may be interested in your product or service, but each may require different strategies when it comes time to close the deal. Emphasize the markets that are most likely to purchase. If you're selling a product or service that's geared toward a specific demographic or industry, it's important to emphasize that fact in your buyer persona profiles.

Prospecting and setting meetings

When it comes to sales enablement training, the gold standard is persistent prospecting. No one wants to be bombarded with emails and phone calls from salespeople they don't know, so your first step is making a connection. Salespeople need to be able to speak confidently about how their product or service has helped other companies before they make the pitch.

With the right sales enablement plan, even the most inexperienced salesperson can become a master of this skill. The following are some tips on how to train your team on effective prospecting techniques:

A solid approach to prospecting begins by focusing on three pillars: making a connection, getting someone's attention, and assuming someone's pain points so that you can offer assistance. You should prepare salespeople with case studies of how particular messages resulted in sales opportunities. This will help them determine what to say and what not to say when seeking new leads. Additionally, it will give them confidence as they prepare for their first cold call or email.

There are many touchpoints through which your reps can interact with potential customers—email, phone calls, direct mail, etc. Make sure that your reps have adequate time to hone their skills in each area. With so many potential touchpoints, it's important that your team feel comfortable with every aspect of their contact with prospective clients.

Improving the quality of demonstrations

The sales demo is a tried-and-true method of helping prospects visualize how your solution will work for their business. But if you're looking to make your demonstrations more effective in the new year, it's time to start training salespeople on how to give a stronger presentation.

Creating an engaging presentation for prospects involves a whole lot more than just talking about features and benefits. It's about showcasing your company's top talent and putting forward the best face of your business. A well-executed demo will let prospects know that working with you will be a pleasure, not just an everyday part of doing business.

So how can you ensure that all those demos are moving in the right direction?

The first step is to outline what makes for a productive discussion. Sales reps need to know what questions to ask and what types of answers they should expect to receive from prospects. The best way to get that information is by talking with your salespeople. You can also look at past presentations, listen to recordings of past demos and review feedback from customers who have used the product.

Then, walk them through the process of preparing a presentation, including creating an outline, outlining their message, and choosing the proper structure and visuals that match the client's needs. The most effective way to do this is by explaining the nuts and bolts of what should be included in the demo presentation and how it should be delivered. A thorough outline of the most common use cases, verticals, and business needs will serve as a strong foundation for each representative's customized presentation.

Finally, they should practice their delivery with some mock roleplay so they can get comfortable with what it's like to give a finished presentation that covers all their bases. Roleplaying with fellow salespeople is an effective way of getting reps to become confident in their delivery and improve their ability to answer questions and objections that may arise during a real discussion with a prospect.

Overcoming objections and winning against competition

In order to train your team on the best strategies for closing deals, you'll want to make sure that they're familiar with both your own company and its rivals. Competitive analysis goes beyond simply learning about the strengths and weaknesses of your competitors. It helps salespeople understand how their company is different from the competition, and how that difference will be useful in overcoming objections.

This analysis should include information on how you compete with other brands in nearly every area of your product or service, from pricing to user experience. It should also looks at the strengths and weaknesses of your competition, as well as how they could react to certain marketing or advertising campaigns. Salespeople must also learn about your strategies for beating out other businesses—for example, providing invaluable customer support when their clients need it most. Competitive analysis will arm them with everything they need to respond effectively when a client brings up a competitor during negotiations. They'll know what questions to ask, what arguments they should make, and more.

Distributing this information allows them to take this knowledge into account when making their pitches. They'll also be better prepared to handle situations where a client brings up a competitor during negotiations—if they know what strengths are important to your clients, they'll have more options for dealing with those situations.

Effectively sharing anecdotes

The best salespeople are great storytellers, so consider giving them plenty of practice time with simulated calls to prospects before sending them out to meet with real ones. You can use this to your advantage when presenting your use cases, as it will increase the likelihood that they will demonstrate differentiation and ultimately result in a sale.

One of the most important aspects of sales enablement is using customer testimonials. Customer testimonials provide social proof, which is the idea that a potential buyer will be more confident in purchasing your product if they know that other people are happy with it.

When you're sharing these case studies with potential clients, it's crucial to make sure that you are presenting them appropriately. The best way to do this is by telling stories about your customers' success with your product, rather than simply trying to convince prospects that your product is superior based on the features alone.

This approach will work best when you have some practice time beforehand; consider conducting fake calls with your sales team so they can get used to presenting their own use cases effectively. This will also increase their confidence and improve their ability to differentiate from competitors before meeting real customers.

Chapter Seven

Content Management

Sales enablement is a critical component of any sales strategy. A lack of marketing and sales content stifles the process of moving prospects through your pipeline, ultimately impeding sales results. The key to overcoming this obstacle is to create a thorough and consistent marketing campaign that provides you with the ability to nurture leads through the entire buying process. When you create content, you're establishing a dialogue with your prospects and giving them information that helps them make informed decisions. In order to effectively do this, however, you need to be able to clearly articulate your value proposition—there can't be any confusion about what you can offer that will justify your customers spending their hard-earned money on it.

If you have a clear, compelling value proposition, you can attract leads and guide them through your sales funnel with effective content marketing—but if you don't, they will be more likely to pass you by or drop out of your pipeline altogether.

Your buyers' buying cycles should be reduced so that they can move quickly and confidently through your sales funnel—and the best way to do that is by showing them exactly what they want to see. You'll need innovative content campaigns that are clear about how your product or service meets their specific needs. Your buyers can't find this information by themselves, so it's up to you to deliver it where they're looking.

So, who is responsible for making sure that each prospect receives all the information she needs when she needs it? The answer: the sales enablement department. Sales enablement professionals are responsible for producing and optimizing the content that prospects need along every step of their buying cycle.

Enablement vs. Marketing Content

There is a lot of overlap in the way your company's marketing and sales materials are written, with the one major difference being that the former often appeals to a broad audience while the latter is tailored to individual buyers. For example, a promotional brochure will be largely written to appeal to the masses—it might mention specific benefits that any customer could get from your product or service, or perhaps how you can save time for everyone. One for salespeople would have much of the same information but would also include language and examples aimed at getting one person on board.

The goal of your sales enablement content, on the other hand, should be to close the loop started by your marketing materials. If your brochure mentioned that you can save time, then your sales rep can take this opportunity to show how exactly you do that—specifically for this buyer whose chief concern was time management. The buyer will immediately see how your product will solve their problem, which will likely cement them as a loyal customer.

Additionally, sales content is tailored to the specific stage of the buyer's journey that the reader currently occupies.

Content tends to follow one of two patterns: the awareness stage (the very top of your funnel) and the consideration stage (the middle of your funnel). It's important to keep these different stages in mind when you're crafting your sales content. The goals and methods for creating an advertisement are very different from those used to create a piece of sales content—which also means that they'll be presented differently.

Content intended for the awareness stage will have a much more direct tone than that intended for the consideration stage.

The goal of content at the awareness level is to get people thinking about a topic, opening their minds to new ideas, and raising questions that could lead them down your sales funnel. The goal of content at the consideration level will be to close this loop by providing answers to questions raised earlier in the buyer's journey.

Creating & Managing Content

When it comes to sales enablement, content management is the first and most crucial step. For a rep to be successful they need to be able to quickly access the right content at the right time. This requires a great deal of planning and consideration in order to ensure that your company is creating valuable content that can be easily found and accessed by sales reps.

There's obvious value in creating awesome content: you're giving your reps knowledge and information that their customers will find useful, thereby building trust and credibility with leads. Studies have shown that less than 60% of the content created for sales is actually being used, which is largely because of the two problems mentioned above: not enough quality/value, and rep's inability to find/use said content.

Sales enablement needs to make sure that this doesn't happen at their organization by focusing on both value and making sure reps are able to access all relevant content.

Consider how many different kinds of content are needed for sales reps at each stage of the funnel: demo scripts for early-stage leads and prospects; educational pieces on product features or use cases for mid-stage leads; high-level overviews and competitive comparisons for late-stage customers up for renewal. If you're not creating these kinds of assets, you're leaving a lot of revenue on the table—and potentially losing out on higher-quality deals that are more likely to renew.

Offer Content at Every Stage of the Buying Process

Content is the backbone of the sales process. It's what makes the sales team stand out from the competition. More than 80% of B2B buyers find content valuable in their purchasing process (CMI, 2016), and 89% of B2B businesses that produce more content than their peers are likely to meet or exceed revenue goals (Salesforce, 2015).

Content enables a sales team to generate leads that are more likely to convert; however, without a content sales strategy, your conversion rates can suffer. Content marketing is not very effective if you don't have a plan for how your company will keep capitalizing on it.

Content should be unique for each customer. Every piece of content generated through content marketing should be segmented for each lead based on their individual needs and the stage of the buying process they're in. Your lead might not even need your product at all! They might just need some information on how to fix some long-standing problem they've been dealing with.

Your job is to figure out what that problem is and provide each prospect with information on how to solve it for themselves or direct them to someone who can offer them a solution (and maybe even become a new lead down the line).

Your job, as sales enablement, is to figure out what that problem is and provide each prospect with information on how to solve it for themselves or direct them to someone who can offer them a solution (and maybe even become a new lead down the line).

If you're looking to improve your sales team's ability to nurture leads, there are several things you should consider. The first is that you should talk to marketing so you can get your hands on the proper tools. Just because your salespeople have access to social media, email and other digital tools doesn't mean they can use them in a way that will help your company's marketing efforts.

Marketers have the skills needed for creating and distributing content, but there are benefits to letting representatives use these tools. Salespeople can leverage the growing trend of content marketing by using social media, blogs and email for longer messages, helping them to communicate about the value of their product or service rather than simply pitching it. This personalization can be crucial for nurturing a lead from one stage of the funnel to another.

It's important to coordinate your sales and marketing efforts so that your representatives can effectively nurture leads at any point in the sales funnel. If they're able to tailor their message based on where the lead is in their buying journey, they'll be able to present your company's products and services in a way that resonates with each audience member and makes them feel more connected with your brand.

Types of Sales Enablement Content

These are some of the commonly produced content for sales enablement.

Competitor Research and Analysis

To continue to grow and succeed in today's highly competitive marketplace, brands must be aware of how their competition is interacting with consumers. In order to remain competitive and keep sales teams up-to-date on the latest trends in their industry, companies must create a culture of analysis that encourages competitors to be studied and monitored.

A well-executed competitor analysis can help sales professionals gain a deeper understanding of the ways in which their company is performing relative to the competition. This information is vital for building a strong business case for a sales pitch. Salespeople who are equipped with information about the ways in which they can improve upon their competition's offerings will be more effective at convincing prospects of the value of their product or service.

Salespeople have an easier time closing deals for the company when they know what their competition is doing and where they're falling short. Competitors' products are constantly evolving and changing, so a sales rep needs to keep up with all of this information so that he or she can stay up-to-date on trends in the market and bring customers the best product for their needs.

Salespeople also have advantage when they are aware of how the competition is interacting with its target audience. If a company knows how its rivals interact with customers, it can come up with ways to stand out from competitors and attract interest from potential customers in its product or service.

Competitor research and analysis content includes comparison charts, graphics, and surveys that educate sales professionals on how to sell a specific product or service to a customer. This type of content helps salespeople build rapport with potential customers by showing them that they are capable of listening to their needs and helping them come up with solutions to meet those needs.

Case Studies

Developing case studies is an essential part of sales enablement content. A prospect is much more likely to become a customer when they see a case study (or a few) that speaks directly to them.

Sales and marketing can work together to develop case studies that help prospects identify with the product and make it more memorable. If a prospect is in the market for a solution, the last thing they're looking for is an abstract pitch that doesn't speak to their problems.

There are two ways your company can develop case studies: either marketing develops them in-house, or sales can help identify current customers who are the biggest champions of your product.

Both teams should be involved in this process — it's easier to take a customer's use of your product and turn it into something digestible than it is to have marketing try to understand how your customers use the product on their own. Marketing needs to develop a vast number of case studies that speaks to every kind of client you have, whether it's by industry, company size, or specific use case. Sales can help identify current customers who are the biggest champions

The best sales enablement content will typically detail the problem that needed fixing, how the company or organization intervened to make things better, and the end result of using the service or product in question. If a late-stage prospect needs convincing that your solution will be a game-changer for them, these materials are invaluable resources.

The salesperson who already knows their target prospect's problem and how they intend to solve it will now have an additional tool to convince them that what they're offering is just what they've been looking for.

Sales Playbooks

A sales playbook is a compilation of strategies, tactics, and tricks that are designed to help a sales team close deals. A sales playbook is essentially a reference manual that details successful sales strategies for a wide range of scenarios.

The playbook can be used to address common obstacles that might arise in the closing process, such as objections or concerns about the product. It also helps teams avoid common mistakes and provides them with templates that they can use to create more effective proposals.

A sales playbook enables the sales team to think strategically about how to approach potential customers, how to make an impact, how to best position their product, and how to close the deal. Salespeople need to be able to rely on proven strategies in order to deliver results consistently. This type of content can help them succeed in their jobs.

In order for the marketing team to create effective educational content, it is crucial that sales leaders sit down with them to share their insights and experiences. The onus then shifts to the marketing group to incorporate the data into concise, simple copy. This can be achieved by using short phrases and sentences in typical conversation format rather than long blocks of text; this will make it easier for readers' eyes to follow along as they read.

Sales Scripts

By providing sales professionals with sales scripts, you are ensuring that your brand is consistent across all channels, including the phone and email. Sales enablement content is how your team will learn to deliver information in the same way that it will be received by prospects.

The key here is to make sure that your content is not only doing its job by providing your team with information they can use to sell your products, but also making sure it doesn't become a hindrance to their success. If a script or piece of content sounds robotic, it won't be useful for your team. Sales professionals need to sound like themselves—informed, helpful and trustworthy—to keep their prospects engaged in the conversation.

Sales scripts should be a guide that help sales professionals get through the conversation with ease. If a sales script is not engaging or if it is too detailed, it will be hard to use effectively and may end up being tossed aside in a sales professional's desk drawer, never to be seen again. Sales scripts drive consistency across the sales funnel by providing a uniform way for team members to approach prospects, while also providing fresh angles on information already provided.

It is crucial for marketers to actively participate in conversations related to sales scripts so they can better understand what is working and what needs improvement.

Explanation Videos

If you're going to be working with a sales team, giving them the ability to do their jobs more effectively is a way to make sure that they have every opportunity to succeed. That's where video becomes an essential tool in your arsenal, because it allows you to demonstrate the product in action and explain how it works.

Video demonstrations are an invaluable resource for sales enablement, because they can bring an abstract concept to life in a way that written content cannot. They can also help provide more information about product features and functions than would be possible in a document.

It has become increasingly apparent that people are looking for more than just simple explanations. They want videos that show them exactly how to do something—that's why there are so many tutorials on YouTube and other sites with millions of views.

While these kinds of videos can be time-consuming to produce (and therefore costly), they are incredibly effective because they clearly show how something is done, so there is no room for misunderstanding.

White Papers

White papers make ideal content for sales enablement, but they can also serve as competitive intelligence or in-depth case studies. They are used for many different purposes for a variety of audiences.

White papers are one of the best options for learning about your industry, but they're also useful for gaining clients' trust and turning them into loyal customers. If you've got a white paper that will teach your salespeople how to do their job more effectively, you should definitely include it on your list of sales enablement content.

White papers are an excellent way to learn something new, and they're also a great way to convince potential clients that they can trust your expertise. When you make use of white papers, you're using the most academically-supported type of content available.

There's no questioning a white paper's credibility because it's all facts, figures, statistics, and personal accounts—it's information that's been thoroughly researched and recorded through scientific means, so you don't have to worry about someone misleading you or trying to give you a sales pitch in place of facts. With that said, white papers will be more effective when they're used as supplementary content rather than as the only thing in your sales enablement arsenal—don't try to convert clients solely with a white paper!

Instead, it should be seen as part of your company's overall strategy; once you've established yourself as an expert, your white paper should serve as proof that what you say is true—it can help you gain the trust of potential clients and give them a sense of security when they're considering your products or services.

Sales Proposals

The proposal is one of the most important aspect of sales enablement content. It's the document that you use to sell a product or service to a client, and it will end up determining whether or not your company gets the contract.

Proposals are written documents that advertise a product or service to possible clients. However, these are unlikely to be successful unless you provide in-depth information about your company, customers (including testimonials from those customers), services, and rates.

When you're writing a proposal, you need to make sure that it looks interesting to the reader. You can do this by justifying your solution—a great idea that many companies overlook. Justifying your solution shows the reader how your service could benefit them without talking down to them or trying to "sell" them on it. This can make your proposal stand out from the rest that your potential clients receive.

Sales Presentations

A strong sales presentation is the bedrock of any successful sales program. It sets you apart from the competition, leaves a positive impression on potential customers, and—most importantly—helps you win new clients.

The objective of a sales presentation is to not only present your company but its value proposition in such a way that it prompts them to buy what you're selling—and maybe more importantly, makes you look like a professional and competent individual.

A successful sales presentation sets the tone for all subsequent interactions with those customers. It sets you apart from the competition and leaves a positive impression on customers that they'll remember long after the details of your products or services have slipped their mind.

A successful presentation will have three components: your delivery (your body language, tone of voice, and speaking skills), your content (what you say and show to support your pitch), and your design (the look of your slides).

Webinars

Webinars are a great way for companies to educate and engage their customers. These online seminars for your business can take many forms: Q&A sessions with an expert, feedback sessions on upcoming features, or demonstrations of how to use a tool. One of a webinar's biggest advantages is that the host is in complete control over the presentation. The audience watches the webinar and listens to questions asked by other participants, but they cannot interact with the presenter directly. If you're hosting a webinar as part of your sales enablement strategy, you want to make sure it's engaging enough so that viewers will want to come back for more.

The most engaging webinars are those that teach their viewers how to accomplish something with the product they're presenting. For product-led webinars, it's essential you co-host with product experts. These could be anyone internal such as the product manager or external like a client who uses your tool. Having experts onboard boosts your webinar's credibility.

In order to help you get even more leads from these webinars, make sure that your sales team was involved in creating them. By doing this, they got a front row seat to the pain points and questions their prospective clients might have. It also gives them an opportunity to practice and polish their responses so they could be ready when they helped guide customers through the onboarding process.

Chapter Eight

Internal Communication

Sales enablement encompasses a wide variety of approaches and areas of study: from content management, to tracking content utilization and engagement analytics, to tailoring content at every stage of the buyer's journey, to providing both Sales and Marketing with the tools they need to succeed.

With all these different methodologies and variables in play, it's important to put these plans into action as efficiently as possible. The daily messages you send are crucial to helping your team, learning from one another, improving sales techniques, and closing more business—whether they are outbound messages from the home office to the field or insight and best practice sharing among co-workers.

In order to make sure that your internal communication is reaching those who need it most and being acted upon by those who receive it, you will need a strong process in place. This starts with a solid understanding of your sales team's behaviors, needs, preferences, and behaviors when working on the road or from home. It's vital that you know how best to reach them—and even more important that you realize whether or not this kind of information is really being received by them.

When companies fall short on sales communications, their inability to get their hands on the resources and data they need will prevent them from gaining a comprehensive understanding of their buyers and responding appropriately with relevant content. In other words, they'll be flying blind.

According to SiriusDecisions' research, 82% of decision-makers believe sales reps are unprepared for meetings. When Sales can't get their hands on the resources and data they need, the company's chances of success plummet. But it's not just about making sure Sales people have access to information—the way that information is communicated makes a big difference as well. If Sales can't read through an executive summary or easily understand why Company X is more likely to become a customer than Company Y, then all that time spent gathering the insights will go to waste.

Communication is Key to Sales Enablement

If your sales staff is to be able to convey your company's values and benefits to potential customers, they must be well-informed themselves. Giving them a clear and consistent strategy for internal communication will help ensure that they have the right knowledge to do their job.

It's crucial that you remain consistent with your strategy. Salespeople need a clear set of guidelines so they know what information is expected from them and what is expected from the company. A well-developed strategy for internal communication will allow your staff members to communicate effectively with each other and their customers, while also promoting a sense of unity and understanding throughout your organization.

Major changes to your sales strategy or new hires in the sales department should be shared via email at the earliest convenience. However, when you're just providing updates on your most recent accomplishments, you may want to opt for a format that's more frequent and easier to digest.

Many companies choose to update their teams about sales analytics via a weekly newsletter. This is a good approach, but it does require extra work from you on a regular basis—you need to prepare it every week and then send it along to everyone in your company. If you don't have the time to devote to this kind of regular internal communication, a video update or similar might be a better fit for you.

Outline the Method of Internal Communication

One of the most important steps along the way is choosing which channels to use for communicating with your sales team members. It's crucial to plan ahead for how you'll promote internal content and on what platforms. Choosing the internal communications tools you will employ is also crucial. It's important to remember that various channels are more suited to conveying various messages. Twitter may be a better platform for the rapid spread of breaking news than LinkedIn and Facebook, for example.

The right tools for your organization can't be chosen until after you've settled on your channels. After you've chosen your channels, you should take some time to plan out where each of your sales enablement initiatives will land on those platforms.

It's crucial to plan ahead for how you'll promote internal content and on what platforms. Choosing the internal communications tools you will employ is also crucial. It's important to remember that various channels are more suited to conveying various messages. Twitter may be a better platform for the rapid spread of breaking news than LinkedIn and Facebook, for example.

The right tools for your organization can't be chosen until after you've settled on your channels. Once you've done that, keep in mind: it's not enough to simply use those internal communications tools; it's also important to make sure everyone knows how to use them!

Align Communication Across the Organization

Not all marketing communication is created equal. In fact, it's worth analyzing what types of communication are most effective for which purposes. A strategy that works for one scenario may not be as well suited to another.

For example, your sales force needs information on product development, pricing and new offerings in order to achieve the company's revenue goals. Meanwhile, your customer service team needs the same information but from a different perspective. Your customer service representatives must know about new products and their features so that they can answer questions about those features when customers call in with questions about them.

The key to creating an effective communication strategy is to develop a priority matrix that aligns the goals of each department with those of the business as a whole. A priority matrix is a tool that allows you to clearly see and communicate the relationship between different departments' needs and how they relate to one another. By creating this visual representation, you can identify any potential gaps in your efforts.

As a result, you can be confident that the right information is reaching the right people, which is a major step toward increasing operational efficiency. In addition to improving your internal operations, this strategy also helps reduce friction between different departments by ensuring that they have the same knowledge base.

Through fostering greater teamwork, we can ensure that all members have a common understanding of procedures and are working cooperatively to achieve the same outcomes. This fosters an environment where everyone supports each other's efforts rather than being perceived as competitors for resources and attention from senior management.

By establishing a common language and understanding of the goals, we can ensure that everyone has a shared understanding of their responsibilities and how they relate to one another. This will reduce confusion, frustration and wasted effort when people are working toward similar goals but don't realize that they're doing so.

Employee Engagement & Cross-Functional Collaboration

Salespeople have ample opportunities to engage with prospects, but in order to keep sales cycles moving forward, they will often need to reach out via email. Depending on the relationship the salesperson has with the prospect, there are a wide variety of strategies for reaching out. Besides boosting response rates, this also raises the prospect's likelihood of opening the email.

Salespeople know that it's important to tailor their email communications with customers, and this should be taken into account with internal communication as well. A lot of companies spend a lot of money on training their employees on how to communicate effectively, but then ignore that same training when it comes time for internal communication. They treat internal communication like it's more about telling than listening and sharing.

The easiest way to make sure your employees are getting the right information is to have a designated person responsible for coordinating the flow of information within your organization.

The person in charge of internal communication should be able to coordinate with everyone involved in the company—not just salespeople or customer success teams or other specific groups—in order to provide information relevant to everyone's needs and goals.

As a company grows, so do the number of teams and individuals to keep track of. It's easy for employees to lose sight of their colleagues' work and the goals they're working toward. This is especially true when teams are not aligned with each other or don't share common objectives. It's even more so in organizations with multiple teams working on different projects. Each team is responsible for its own successes, and so each needs to know how to operate independently—but there also needs to be some way of keeping everyone on the same page.

Ideally, internal communications should function as an "enabler" that pushes information out to all relevant parties at the right time. That way, everyone will be able to work together flawlessly and achieve the company's goals in a timely fashion.

This can be challenging because every department has specific requirements and each team that contributes to your "enablement engine" will need its own unique information at different times throughout the process. However, if you can design a system that provides the right information at the right time, everyone will be able to work more efficiently and have a greater impact on your customers.

Chapter Nine

Technology & Tools

Technology has made its way into every part of our lives. It's hard to imagine life without computers, social media, and the internet. Sales enablement technology is no different. It's been around for a while but it's becoming more sophisticated every day.

The modern sales professional's reality is that technology and automation can streamline many of the processes that used to be entirely manual. This is a boon for the whole business, from the first stages of prospecting to the last stages of closing. Many processes that used to be entirely manual can now be automated for sales reps, enabling them to sell better and faster.

In today's age of "always on" everything, salespeople don't have time to look for information on their own. Sales enablement technology gives salespeople access to the content they need in order to be successful. Through automated technology, the sales process is streamlined, allowing customers to spend less time on the phone with unhelpful support staff and more time talking with salespeople who are better able to meet their needs.

Technology Benefits the Customer Experience

Technology is enabling companies to continuously improve their customer experience by providing information that salespeople need in order to influence and convert prospects. By collecting data from a large number of sources, AI can help sales reps identify which products and services customers want, how they want to be communicated with, and what the best time is for engaging with them.

To maintain a consistently high level of customer experience, it's important to make sure that no opportunity for additional content touch points is wasted. In order to keep customers moving as quickly and smoothly as possible through the sales funnel, the right technology can recommend the optimal time to introduce additional content. According to Forbes, up to 95% of customers only buy from companies that provide content throughout the entire sales process. Sales enablement software can tell you if you're falling short.

Using manual analysis or AI-assisted analysis, this kind of software can pinpoint user experience bottlenecks. Brand inconsistencies, low conversion rates, and failing to understand a customer's wants and habits can all be pinpointed, addressed, and tracked with the help of a streamlined management system.

Technology Enables Sales

Sales enablement technology helps to eliminate the need for content silos between sales and marketing. This misalignment is often a challenge, as there is commonly a conflict between marketing qualified leads and sales qualified leads.

Sales enablement technology gives the sales team more control over the customer relationship and the sales process by giving them access to all of the most relevant information about a specific prospect. This can be helpful for sales reps, who can access all relevant information about their prospects in one place, regardless of whether it came from a marketing or sales rep.

Each salesperson or marketer is able to select which content is most relevant at any given time without having to second-guess whether or not it's appropriate to share with the sales team, which eliminates the need for content silos with every vendor having equal access to all information at any time.

Across the board, sales enablement solutions are becoming more prevalent thanks to the advent of more sophisticated technologies in the field. Over the past two decades, salespeople have had to use a combination of various tools and resources to get the materials they need for their job done—the problem is that they were scattered all over the place. In addition to having different formats, these materials were not always up-to-date or tailored to fit the specific needs of each person and his or her specific role.

Sales enablement solutions are designed to help eliminate those inefficiencies by consolidating as many sales-related portals and platforms as possible so that teams can easily access information from a single platform, regardless of its context.

In order to make sure that sales enablement solutions are effective, it's important to put an emphasis on effectiveness, education, and cooperation. To ensure that everyone has everything they need—and nothing more than what they need—to get the job done, it's imperative that everyone involved is well educated about what's available in this content hub. Salespeople should be encouraged to add their own contributions so that data can be consolidated from 60 percent of content that does not originate in marketing (and even further when considering external sources).

Choose the Right Tools

Sales enablement is the tool of choice for today's sales teams. A sales enablement strategy is a method of helping your sales team succeed at the job they were hired to do. It begins with an in-depth understanding of the needs of your sales organization, and then it's implemented with a combination of technology and training to maximize effectiveness.

The best strategy starts with your foundation—that's how you will build your strategy for success. The most important part of building a foundation is figuring out where you can make improvements and then doing that. Sales enablement technology can revolutionize your business, so it's essential that you choose wisely when deciding on which tools to use. The benefits are clear: better customer service and less hassle when using more optimized content strategies.

Sales leaders must be able to evaluate their own organization and determine what resources are needed to help their sales teams succeed, then implement a solution that builds upon these strengths. The technology will empower the existing process, rather than replace it, so it's essential that everyone is involved from the start in order to ensure success.

Generally, you need to consider the following factors when evaluating the tools to use in your sales enablement tech stack:

Ease of use

The easiest way to evaluate ease of use is to test out the product yourself or have someone on your team who has experience with it do so. It's not enough to just look at screenshots or read through the user manual; you need to actually log in and play with it yourself. This will help you understand how straightforward it is to navigate, what kinds of functionality are available, and if you're able to pick up on usage quickly or if it requires training or learning time.

Most importantly, this should give you an understanding of how intuitive the platform is; if your testers struggle with it, that's probably not a good sign. Another useful way to evaluate ease of use is to look at the documentation and support resources available for the product. If there are only a few pages on their website or they don't have any training materials, that could be an indicator that it takes time and effort to learn how to use their software.

Analytics and data

SALES ENABLEMENT

Achieving sales success is an ongoing effort. Sales analytics and data can help you stay on track by tracking performance, identifying trends, and making informed decisions about how to improve your processes. Analytics can also tell you when a plan is working or when you need to make adjustments to improve results. The better armed you are with relevant sales data, the more likely it is that you'll achieve your goals, forecast demand, and identify gaps in your sales funnel.

Sales enablement systems track a lot of data. It's important to know what you want to measure in order to get the most out of your sales analytics.

The biggest mistake companies make when they're just starting to track sales enablement data is that they don't plan ahead. They choose a tool and start tracking data without knowing what they're looking for. The worst part is that they can't figure out why the numbers aren't adding up, because they haven't defined their goals yet.

Before you start looking at tools, take some time to think about what you want your sales enablement program to accomplish. What kind of information will help you better understand the ROI of your initiatives? Which metrics are most important for the success of your sales team? Which trends do you hope to see over time? There are many different types of sales data that can be tracked — some are more relevant than others depending on what your goals are, so it's important to have these questions answered before choosing a system.

Integration with your CRM

To maximize their effectiveness, sales enablement tools should be integrated with your company's CRM software. A CRM, or customer relationship management system, is used to track new leads, store customer data and maintain relationships with clients. A sales enablement tool, on the other hand, provides an overview of the entire sales life cycle.

While a sales enablement platform is certainly a CRM, and vice versa, they serve very different purposes. A sales CRM, or customer relationship management software, is designed to track new leads and store customer data. A sales enablement tool, on the other hand, provides an overview of the entire sales life cycle.

A comprehensive tool will optimize training and content delivery at specific points in the cycle to close more deals. Some programs are specifically designed to integrate smoothly with a number of leading CRMs. If you already have a sales CRM that you love, you may want to consider going with a tool that's been designed with it in mind.

Content creation and management

Sales leaders often complain about inconsistencies in messaging or the availability of content, but consistent and relevant sales content is crucial to winning deals. Knowing where to find the information you need is critical.

Inevitably, though, your team will grow and your needs will change. You might want to reach new markets with a different message. You might want to create new content faster to address changing market conditions or respond to competition. A distinct benefit of a sales enablement software tool that allows employees to create marketing content is that you can quickly scale your impact and address these needs as they arise.

There's always something new to learn about marketing best practices, too—and how they apply to your particular industry or geography. Sales enablement software that includes training content management capabilities can help you keep processes and messaging consistent across all channels, from your flagship website down to social media and beyond.

With sales enablement software, you can create and manage relevant content for your sales team more easily than ever before. By organizing existing assets and streamlining their delivery, such tools enable salespeople to spend more time on high-value activities like building relationships and closing deals. They also help teams stay informed about new trends and developments in the industry, so they can better position themselves to meet the needs of customers—and sell more effectively as a result.

Mobile-friendly

Sales reps are often on the go, and you can't always expect them to be able to access your online content from a desktop computer. Many of today's sales engagement platforms are compatible with mobile devices, which means that reps can engage with your content anytime and anywhere.

Modern sales engagement platforms are designed for mobility in mind. Cloud-based technology allows salespeople to sync notes, files and attachments from anywhere at any time. Sales enablement platforms can be synced to a user's mobile device so that no matter where they are or what they are doing, they can view the latest sales information without effort.

You also want to make sure that your sales engagement platform has features that help make it accessible on mobile devices—features like bookmarking (so sales reps can return to what they were previously viewing) or in-app search capabilities (so they don't have to scroll endlessly through hundreds of articles).

How to Use Technology for Sales Enablement

Sales enablement is all about creating the right sales environment for your team to be successful, so it makes sense that you'd want to make your sales enablement processes as easy as possible. Technology and automation can be two fantastic ways to cut down on the time-intensive parts of sales enablement and allow you to focus your efforts on leadership, strategy, and other roles within your company.

These are four common ways to use technology to drive enablement:

1. Create Email Sequences

2. Automate Sales Prospecting

3. Direct Message Prospects

4. Manage Content and Resources

Create Email Sequences

Sales enablement technology enables sales teams to scale their outreach efforts. It can provide a variety of helpful tools for your team, such as managing prospects, automating lead management and nurturing tools, and creating email sequences.

Many sales enablement tools are focused on prospecting. Use these tools to find new leads and manage your existing ones.

Email-based communication is one of the most popular forms of communication in the business world today, so it's no surprise that multiple sales enablement tools focus on this topic. Find email templates (with personalization tokens) that reps can use to build their own outreach messages so they don't have to start from scratch every time they reach out to someone new.

Set up automated email sequences that will automatically send a series of emails based on certain triggers, such as no response from a prospect after five days. If you have set rules about who should be contacted by which team member when, you could even automate the entire outreach process further.

Automate Sales Prospecting

In order to automate prospecting, sales executives should create links that direct prospects directly to calendar invitations. The link should include the rep's name and industry so that prospects know they have been contacted by someone with expertise in their space. This will allow reps to simply open their calendars every day to find multiple meetings with qualified buyers already there saving them hours of prospecting time.

Salespeople have been using email as a prospecting tool for years, but the amount of time needed for this type of outreach has kept them from using it to its full potential. The next generation of sales enablement tools are taking this to the next level by building automation into their platforms.

Direct Message Prospects

One way to help reps connect with the leads that are most likely to convert is to automate the process. Automated live chat can surface when prospects are most receptive—when they're already on your website—and can help reps close deals faster.

To set up automated live chat, you need a tool that can be customized to send messages based on what information prospects supply at certain stages of the sales cycle. The key is to make sure these automated messages don't appear too soon or too late in the process—if they come too early, they might give prospects the impression that you're just trying to sell them something; if they come too late, they won't be able to have much impact on whether or not a lead converts into a customer.

To ensure your content isn't going out to prospects who aren't really interested in sales enablement content, you can use filtering criteria when setting up automated live chat.

Manage Content and Resources

Sales enablement software is becoming increasingly available for sales teams to help automate the processes of managing content and resources. Sales enablement software provides the ability to create, share, edit, and manage resources and content with ease. This allows your marketing team to easily collaborate with sales on the content they create and share with prospects and customers.

Sales enablement software allows sales teams to manage their content, resources, and materials from a central location. Sales reps can access the information they need at any time and the marketing and sales teams can collaborate seamlessly on the materials they create and share with prospects and customers.

Sales enablement software solutions give you the ability to search all of your content in one place and create or update various types of files in one central location. You can also use these solutions to determine which of your sales reps are using what type of content to ensure that everyone is getting the most from the content you're creating for them.

Even if you've got an extensive collection of content on your site, you want to make sure that it's easy for your sales reps to find exactly what they're looking for when it comes time for them to send an email to a prospect or prepare for a sales call. Sales enablement software allows you to easily organize all of your resources into different categories so that users can search by topic or industry. This ensures that your team members have everything they need at their fingertips.

Chapter Ten

Conclusion

While sales enablement isn't a new concept, it has become increasingly relevant in the last few years as organizations have come to realize that traditional training or out-of-the-box solutions aren't enough to keep salespeople competitive in today's market. Sales enablement is a way for corporations to keep their teams up-to-date on changing trends, engage with customers more efficiently, and provide value for the customer through better selling.

Enablement isn't one thing: it's an entire philosophy of how an organization can support its people. On one hand, there's the technology infrastructure that holds your content and enables you to easily find what you need. On the other hand, there's the culture of support and training throughout your company. These two things are intertwined: a company culture of ownership over sales enablement allows for the creation of effective content that then becomes a resource for onboarding future employees on how best to succeed at work.

www.ingramcontent.com/pod-product-compliance
Lightning Source LLC
Chambersburg PA
CBHW070303220526
45465CB00004B/1728